AF254496

Lunchboxes

Lunchboxes

Poems

Dan Veach

Iris Press
Oak Ridge, Tennessee

Copyright © 2019 by Dan Veach

All rights reserved. No portion of this book may be reproduced in any form or by any means, including electronic storage and retrieval systems, without explicit, prior written permission of the publisher, except for brief passages excerpted for review and critical purposes.

Cover photos are courtesy of the Lunchbox Museum
www.lunchboxmuseum.com

Book Design: Robert B. Cumming, Jr.

Iris Press
www.irisbooks.com

Library of Congress Cataloging-in-Publication Data

Names: Veach, Dan, 1948- author.
Title: Lunchboxes : poems / Dan Veach.
Description: Oak Ridge, Tennessee : Iris Press, [2019]
Identifiers: LCCN 2018051082 | ISBN 9781604542516 (paperback : alk. paper)
Subjects: LCSH: American poetry—21st century.
Classification: LCC PS3622.E33 A6 2019 | DDC 811/.6—dc23
LC record available at https://lccn.loc.gov/2018051082

Acknowledgments

Some of these poems have previously appeared in the following publications:

Bridgewater International Poetry Festival Anthology (Unbound Content, 2018): "Elephant Water"
California State Poetry Quarterly: "The Seal"
Cortland Review: "Millers"
Evansville Review: "Elegy for the Age of Oil"
Humanities Fond (Russia): "My Long Thigh Bone"
Illuminations: "Thanks for the Metaphor"
Light: "Hearing Aids"
Lighten Up Online: "Down on the Sea"
Main Street Rag: "Surprised"
Perfume River Poetry Review: "Redemption"
Sotheby's International Poetry Competition Anthology (Arvon Foundation, 1982): "In Honor of Roaches"
Stone, River, Sky: An Anthology of Georgia Poems (Negative Capability Press, 2015): "Vale of Soles"

"Age of Information" was videotaped and distributed by the University System of Georgia as the GALILEO National Poetry Month presentation for April 2015.

The poems in Section V, as well as "Millers," "Tar Baby," and "The Water Hose," appeared in *Elephant Water* (Finishing Line Press, 2012).

Contents

IV. A Date with Clio
Muse of History

V. A Sprinkling of *Elephant Water*

8

Introduction

Given that my first book, *Elephant Water*, took forty years to finish, and this one came in under seven, I am almost agog at my own blinding speed and efficiency. I did have a deadline this time: the 25th Anniversary of *Atlanta Review*, the international poetry journal I founded with Capers Limehouse and guided for more than two decades. After spending its first twenty years in my spare bedroom, *Atlanta Review* has gone off to college at Georgia Tech, where it is lovingly tended by editor Karen Head, managing editor J.C. Reilly, and a whirring flock of students, interns, postdocs, and faculty advisors. I must say I rather envy it.

The result is, I now have the leisure for what Rossini called "the sins of my old age," among them this lunchbox you've just flipped the latch on. Like every good lunchbox, you'll find a bit of baloney inside, and also, I hope, a slice or two of Wonder bread. Lunch hour will be extra long today: from 1,000,000 BC to the millisecond before *right now*. For those who missed it, there's also a nice cool thermos of *Elephant Water*. Enjoy your lunch!

I would like to thank the Side Door Poets, convened by Karen Paul Holmes, for the sensitive and helpful critiques they've offered over the years. The best advice for any poet is to join or start a good writers' group. Thanks also to Joan Colby, whose bluesy poems about Clio, the muse of history, inspired the "Date with Clio" section in this book. Thanks always to my partner Billie Jean Collins, for caring passionately about my poetry, for giving perceptive advice, and, despite the fact that she wrote the book on that ancient civilization, for being amused by "The Hittites."

Thanks also to Allen Woodall, Jr., founder and director of the Lunchbox Museum in Columbus, Georgia, for allowing us to photograph his unique collection and graciously offering to host the world premier celebration of this book.

It's a special pleasure for me to publish with Iris Press since I spent my high school years in Oak Ridge, Tennessee, and wrote my first poetry there. It's a place where creativity, intellect, and love of nature were always encouraged, and it's gratifying to see that tradition continued with such elegance by Robert and Beto Cumming.

Dan Veach
Decatur, Georgia
2018

I.   Lunchboxes

Superman Capes

Faster than a speeding bullet,
gifted with glorious powers,
we leaped over sidewalk cracks
at a single bound. We'd play for hours

rushing about with our arms stretched out
singing the Superman song.
It didn't tax the memory too much,
being just one word long:

Superman! Superman!
Superman, Superman, Superman!

We didn't need a big red "S"
or biceps to bulge and flex.
We got our superpowers from the towels
we tied around our necks.

That intoxicating cape!
Just like a magician would wear,
pulling mysterious, crackling energy
out of the empty air.

We felt that any moment we could fly.
Let older heads than ours debate
whether we could levitate—
we needed no *how* and no *why*.

Equally amazed at everything,
not having learned or been taught,
who were we to know or say
if this world was magic or not?

Coonskin Caps

were a bit of the wild, wooly East
for kids like us, living out West
in tame little L.A. housing tracts
without any trees or beasts.

My claim to Disney's Daniel Boone
and Davy Crockett was as good as any:
my Mom from backwoods Tennessee,
my Dad from the hills of Kentucky.

Fluffy ring-tails swinging,
Johnny and Bobby and I made a desperate stand
behind our driveway's redwood fence
with long sticks instead of long rifles.

We fended off the ferocious attacks
of my three-year-old sister, Maida—
that little blonde pixie was the only one
we could convince to be the Mexicans.

While Santa Ana's cannons roared,
our rifles went "Pow!" and "Keew!"
our labial and fricative explosions
decimating his savage horde.

Much later, in San Antonio, I realized
we had some advantages over the Alamo:
a narrow approach, a shorter wall, a foe
who wandered about in a daze.

Still, with three more young Crocketts
decked out in coonskin caps, I have to say
things might have gone better for Texas
had we fought with Davy that day.

Forts

Crusader castles on mountain crags,
log stockades of the U.S. Cavalry,
the gentle adobe curves of the Alamo—
how we loved them as little boys.

When we were weak, wide open
and soft to the bone
how we longed, like hermit crabs
for those safe, solid shells
of timber and rock and stone.

Closed spaces with narrow slits
in their turrets and battlements
where a boy, armed only
with a bow and arrow
or a BB gun, could hold
the whole howling world at bay.

Guns & Holsters

Why did I want them so desperately?
Two shiny six-shooters with plastic handles,
a gun belt with silver studs
and holsters trimmed in leather fringe.
I was just five, but my deepest desires
would make any pacifist cringe.

Of course, I'd seen guns on TV—
no one who ever poked a cow
would be caught dead without one.
In the old lawless West they were
the one friend you could count on.
They turned a boy into a man.

But a *naked* gun was just an embarrassment:
Stick it in your belt, you'd risk
shooting yourself in the foot—or worse.
Only a shifty Mississippi gambler
would hide his weenie Derringer
in a pocket or a purse.

No, you had to have a holster—
hoarse and emphatic, a manly word—
made of equally tough and manly leather.
And who would even think
of wearing one in white, or pink?
Black and brown were the only decent colors.

Red rolls of caps made all the bangs louder
and gave me my first whiff of real gunpowder.
You had to be quick on the draw—
over and over, I practiced pulling them out
and, after a pop and a fancy spin,
putting them back in again.

When you've got a gun, the bad guys
are suddenly lurking everywhere.
You may not see them, but they're there,
hiding in ambush behind the shrubbery.
I could hear rustlers, rustling the leaves
of my Aunt Ruth's rubber tree.

Sadly, I lived in the new, law-abiding West.
Still, if Black Bart ever dared
to crawl out of the TV set, I was prepared.
In a shootout, I would never run.
I could defend my friends and family now,
the Boy with the Silver Gun.

The Good Humor Man

On our long, hot summer afternoons
how we looked forward to that truck
with its merry, tinkling tunes.
The Good Humor Man!

Such a quaintly old-fashioned name.
Of the four English *humours*
that made up men's moods
he had only one—

always *sanguine*, rosy-cheeked
and full of cheer. No excess
of cold black bile, the cause
of *melancholy*, nor yet that hot

and furious yellow choler. How could
you be *choleric*, surrounded by stacks
of cool white ice cream bars?
Salivating, yes, but not *phlegmatic*,

we eagerly raced to beg our mothers
for dimes and nickels for popsicles—
grape and cherry, lemon, lime—
was it time yet, was it time?

As the jingling grew ever nearer
we bounced up and down on tiptoe,
anxious, afraid we might miss
our one chance at afternoon bliss—

little physicians, desperate to bring
our hot, dry *humours* into balance
with something wet and cool as an English spring—
our own sweet medicine for melancholy.

Sidewalk Horses

*Vikings used to call their ships
the horses of the sea.*

In our dreams we had horses:
Palominos like Roy Rogers' Trigger
Black Beauties with stars on their foreheads
the Lone Ranger's white stallion, Silver
galloping over the vast desert wasteland
of 1950s black-and-white TV.

In real life, we had bikes.
Schwinns, Murrays, and J.C. Higgins—
these were our horses of the sidewalk
galloping over the concrete deserts
and asphalt wastelands of our once-wild West.

We would go nowhere without them,
not even the neighbors' next door.
Putting all our mettle to the pedal,
our feet scarcely touched the ground—
walking was far too pedestrian
for *caballeros* such as we.

We would pet and encourage our mounts
as though they had flying manes and heaving flanks.
But we put our own beating hearts, our soul and sweat
into those rubber-shod steeds, their whirling cranks—
propelling ourselves as fast as we could dare
cooled by the breeze we made ourselves
our own wind running wildly through our hair.

Writing

"I know how to write!"
a kindergarten friend confided.

I was agog, astounded—
writing was some kind of secret
that only the grownups knew.

"You do not!" I scoffed.

"I've seen them do it!" he insisted,
and pulling out pencil and paper
slowly inscribed this mysterious line:

mmmmmmmmmmmmmmmmmmmmm

"That's it?" I muttered,
shocked and disappointed.

This was the great big secret
we were supposed to learn in school?

This was how our elders spent their hours,
staring at this stupid stuff all day?

"Grownups!" I sniffed, disgusted.
"What do *they* know, anyway?"

Lunchboxes

Exiled in an alien country,
these were our only vestiges
of home—a secret message
encrypted in peanut butter
and purple jelly, baloney
and yellow mustard, written
on white Wonder Bread.

Tin boxes, shiny and thin
with rattling plastic handles,
illumined in reds and yellows
to banish our homesick blues
with pictures of heroes and friends—
Superman and Wonder Woman
Davy Crockett, Daniel Boone
Donald and Daffy Duck.

Apples and oranges rumbled within,
a thermos to keep our milk cool
and something that brightened our mood—
what would be hidden there today,
light, spongy Twinkies
or dark Hostess cupcakes,
angel or devil's food?

Amid all the concrete and schoolyard din,
each was a gift from above
concealing a heart of pure white cream
as sweet and secret as a mother's love.

I was a Lord, very briefly

My second-grade "gang"
was just three guys, whose loyalty
was bought with candy cigarettes,
glass marbles, Pez dispensers, bubble gum,
baseball and football trading cards
(though not my Duke Snyder
or Crazylegs Hirsch, of course).

Only when reading *Beowulf* much later
did I learn how a Lord was supposed to act,
freely and gladly giving out treasure—
swords and armor, gold and silver rings—
rewarding the valiant deeds of his vassals.

My vassals were never valiant,
never did anything at all, in fact
except ask me for more and more stuff.
The last straw was the golden eagle clasp
from my Cub Scout neck kerchief.

At that, I said "Enough!"
The fact is, I was just too cheap
to be a Lord. Generosity
did not run in my Scottish blood—
only the oatmeal I ate each morning,
the breakfast, not of Champions,
but of misers.

That, and the fact my allowance,
a miserly quarter a week,
could only buy so much loyalty
even at 1950s prices
when gas was a quarter a gallon.

No, I was not cut out to rule a fief,
to hear men say *my liege.*
Fed up with my onerous role,
I breathed a big sigh of relief
when the burden of *noblesse oblige*
was lifted at last from my second-grade soul.

Paradise Fumbled

Better to reign in Hell, than serve in Heaven.
—Satan, in Milton's *Paradise Lost*

My second-pick football teams,
the chubby, the awkward,
the guys with glasses,
always got knocked on their asses

unless I played quarterback.
My dream was to be a receiver,
catching instead of throwing passes.
But Fate dropped me into a different slot.

QB—the job the glory hogs
all wanted, throwing the long bombs,
soaring spirals everyone admired
but no one could ever catch.

My plan was different.
Wracked with anxiety, the CEO
of split-second decisions,
I threw short, easy lobs

that even my luckless crew
couldn't possibly muddle.
"Go out five steps, then turn around!"
was the play I called in every huddle.

We marched to touchdown after touchdown,
losers exulting at last in victory. Great fun
for everyone but the quarterback, harassed
by pass defenders, burdened with responsibility.

Pride was my downfall. Unlike Lucifer,
that brilliant devil, I didn't care
to be the star, to feel the flaming heat.
My sin was that I couldn't bear defeat.

On that field of broken dreams
I had to choose. To catch or throw
the football? To lose in Heaven,
or to win in Hell?

Thanks for the Metaphor

Oak Ridge High School, Tennessee

Third period gym class
was his cross to bear.
Our moans and groans
were fit to make Coach tear
his thinning hair out.

It was only fair, he thought
to have a little harmless fun—
he'd make us run the Mile for time,
untrained, unwitting, unprepared.

"Boys, you can do it—
you're all *young!*"
he said, to incredulous stares.
"It's just four laps around the track.
Wait for the starting gun—"
(*and say your prayers*).

We're off! And at the first turn, out of breath.
None of us knew what four laps meant,
how to set a survivable pace.
Like a pack of fools, we ran flat out
from the very get-go of the race.

Second lap,
we're flat-out winded.
Legs are heavy, wooden,
spirits low.
Nothing left,
and half the race to go.

Third lap is a memory
the decades do not dim.
Somewhere on the other side of pain
I found myself strangely at sea:
Floating lightly in the sunny air
on a peaceful tropic island far removed
from my lungs, my legs, my body's misery.

Fourth lap: the final turn in sight,
a second Inspiration came.
A Divine Wind we had never known
revived our spirits and propelled
our Kamikaze mission to its end.

Coach was no Einstein.
When he sent us orbiting in outer space
we came back, somehow, older
than the boys we left behind.
Men, he called us for the first time
when we crossed that finish line.

Every day has its afternoon,
every week the wait for Friday.
Every year has its dreary season,
every winter, February.
Spring and morning disappear
with a regularity that's stunning.
Then I think to myself: *Third lap*.
And keep on running.

Millers

Small, unassuming, dusty gold,
their wings swept back like jets,
we called them "millers"
years before I heard
of human mills and millers.
Little skippers built for speed,

you had to be lucky and lightning quick
to catch one. When released,
they left a fairy powder
on our fingers, flecks of gold
more finely divided than dust.
I knew what it meant to catch a fleeting thing

before they ever taught me how to grind
the flour of the word. Before I ever heard
of Chaucer's miller, windmills,
Don Quixote's reckless charge—
before I ever threw myself, headlong
against the whirling beauty of the world.

Tar Baby

Southern California, 1958

It was the 50s: the American Mesozoic.
Oil well pumps, like friendly dinosaurs
nodded drowsily all day
as we whizzed by on black asphalt roads
in our own gas-guzzling prehistoric beasts:

Plymouths, Ramblers, DeSotos, Giant Pink
Cadillacs roamed the tar-black land,
flew past on pterodactyl fins—
to my 10-year-old eyes
the most beautiful creatures on earth.

Asphalt erupted from the ground, volcanic, lava-like.
Black pavement and parking lots engulfed
the orange groves and eucalyptus trees—
they were transplants anyway, while tar
was homegrown, natural, organic.

Blacktop suited our antiseptic age:
nobody trusted dirt
or the things that grew there.
Uncle Leo, who worked at the plastic factory,
warned us to wash our hands, or we'd get "Germans."

Like Br'er Rabbit, tar was our baby.
Asphalt playgrounds were my meadows fair.
White lines on blacktop ruled my life—
my baseball diamond, football gridiron,
dodgeball circle, foursquare square.

On school field trips, we went to see the Tar Pits
at La Brea, L.A.'s ancient Mesozoic zoo.
Strange but true: mammoths and sabertooth tigers,
glyptodonts, a pet shop full of prehistoric beasts
got stuck here, just like us, in the tarry goo.

An age long passed. Both of us tar baby divorcées,
Br'er Rabbit and I now live in a briar patch
Back East. But the saber tooth of memory
still gnaws my bones today—stuck
in the timeless tar pits of L.A.

The Water Hose

Magical snake
in the grass
of our tract house Eden,
writhing with sudden
life, speaking in cool
clear tongues
that only children understood.

How you spewed out
your rubbery blessings,
preaching to the choir
of innocents
sermons of splash and scream—
all of us leaping,
squealing in fearful glee.

Southern California, hot
asphalt streets and concrete
sidewalks, little lawns,
no shade from trees—just you
and us, all summer long
while all the grownups hid indoors
we children watered ourselves
and grew like weeds.

II.   KINFOLK & FAMILY

Grandpa's House

A place of profound mystery
for a kid who, except for some spindly palms
had scarcely seen a tree.

In the deep woods of Tennessee,
built of weathered gray boards, a chimney
of stone, a long porch with rocking chairs.

Grandpa Garrett offered us a drink
from a metal dipper in a metal pail
of earthy water hauled up from his well.

Inside, the smells of aging wood
and smoke. A black cast iron stove
with split logs stacked beside it.

Blackberries and blue-green June bugs,
a pond overgrown with cattails, overrun
with cottonmouth moccasin snakes.

Nature calls even city kids—
they showed me the path to the outhouse,
winding through waist-high weeds.

Inside, a rough wooden board with a hole,
a Sears Roebuck catalog
and, oddly, a few scattered corn cobs

whose purpose I never guessed
until the day I overheard
my mother say *That cobs me!*

That evening I walked over windfalls
under a dark and twisted apple tree.
Its fruit was scary: wormy, knobby

greenish yellow flecked with brown,
unlike the big red apples, smooth and round
we got at the grocery store.

But one rough crunch, wild to the core
gave me a taste for Tennessee, and tamer fruit
would never be Delicious any more.

Doc

Young Amos Walter Garrett's dream
was to be a doctor.
The odds were stacked against him,
coming from a one-room school
in remote, rural Tennessee.

Still, he had his bags all packed
for the long ride to college in Nashville
when his mother suddenly burst into tears
and begged him not to leave her.
He set his suitcase down.

Became, like his father, a farmer.
Barn builder, plowman, cattle drover—
whatever anyone needed, he was,
including a rough country medic.
His neighbors called him "Doc."

One of his seven daughters, Anna Lee
was paralyzed by a strange disease
the doctors couldn't diagnose or cure.
Was it desperation or deep country lore
that made him feed more and yet more
raw hog's liver to his dying daughter?

Unlike Poe's Annabel Lee, my mother
was soon chasing June bugs again with her sisters.
Mom would be fond of hog liver all her life,
much to her children's disgust.

Three city doctors won the Nobel Prize
for discovering, later on, that liver
was the cure for pernicious anemia,
before then a fatal disease.

Doc could have told them that.
But his tree had fallen deep in the forest
of Tennessee's oaks and pines,
and no one had ever heard it—
except for my mom and, later on
her child who wrote these lines.

Taking Reva Home

One year the trip Back East
took on a more serious tone.
Mom and Dad talked
in the front seat of the Ford
about things we had little clue of.

Reva, the youngest of Mom's seven sisters
stayed home to take care of their father.
But Grandpa had taken to drinking moonshine
and taking his shotgun to the boys
who came to court her. Once, Mom whispered,
while Reva was washing dishes
he'd hugged her from behind.

This time, when we left Tennessee
Reva was coming with us.
Sitting in a cane chair on his porch
Grandpa was waving goodbye
when he suddenly cradled
his head in his hands
and began sobbing bitterly.

Let me out!
Reva cried.
I can't leave him like this!

Mom was silent.
Daddy kept on driving.

Aunt Reva Takes a Dip

On our way West
we drove through the desert for days.
Though Mom tried to discourage
her sister's country ways,
Aunt Reva was still dipping snuff
keeping her dark brown drool
in a bright red Coca-Cola cup.

Route 66 through Arizona
in the days before air conditioning:
Bugs splatting their yellow insides
on the windshield, a wet burlap water bag
hanging over our blazing radiator.

Opening windows did no good—
only let in a furnace blast
that might have melted steel.
Still, I and my sister insisted,
too antsy to sit there and bake.

This turned out to be a mistake.
Aunt Reva, sitting up front
seized on the opportunity, and spit
a mouthful of snuff, which unexpectedly
was sucked back inside the rear window
all over Maida and me.

In California, Reva got a job
and met a man at the plastic factory
who shortly became Uncle Leo.
Mom and Dad were delighted
when Leo got Reva to give up snuff
and take up smoking—
a modern, stylish, sanitary habit.

Father and the Forward Pass

for David Bottoms,
whose father favored the bunt

My father favored the forward pass,
or better said, he threw them as a favor
to his 10-year-old son
whose greatest joy in life
was catching footballs.

Sundays we spent with Aunt Ruth
and Uncle Joe, whose greatest joy
was grilling steaks on his big brick barbecue.
In the long afternoons after lunch
(T-bones and iced tea for grownups,
hamburgers and RC Cola for the kids)
Dad and I always played catch.

I would hike him the ball, then bolt
from the scrimmage line—
quick cuts eluding imaginary foes—
stretch out ahead to snag a pass
then, trotting back, toss it to him.
I was tireless, a receiver
as eager as a Labrador retriever,
and Dad's patience had no end.

My hero was Raymond Berry,
wide end for the champion Colts
who would run up to strangers on the street
even old ladies, little kids, and ask them
to throw him a pass. Too bad
he never got to meet my dad.

Unlike Uncle Joe,
who was built like a brick barbecue,
Dad was too slight and skinny
to go out for football in high school.

But he had the touch.
He knew how to lead his man,
to throw the ball into the future—
not where I was
but where I was going to be.

Father and the Buddha

He was always anxious,
screwed up tight
by a twisted spine,
one shoulder blade
protruding from his back.

And so it was almost a mercy
when the small strokes began
that loosened his mind,
made him more sociable, more at ease,
less worried what others would think.

But now his heart was failing too
after a long life, the doctor said,
given the shape he was in.

There was no struggle at the end.
He lay back in bed—and then
for the first time in my life
I saw my father's face relax.

A comely change at first,
an assurance I had never seen till now.
But then his calm grew deeper still
as all human care and caring
ebbed away from the shoreline of his brow.

At last he looked as peaceful as the Buddha.
And I, who had always admired
such Eastern stillness, such tranquility
recoiled from it now in horror.

How I yearned for my father's care,
his fear, his worry, his anxiety.
How much more precious they were to me
than this perfect calm, this stark serenity.

The burdens that bent his back so long
had been lifted, every one
and now settled slowly, cool and dark
upon his only son.

Mother and the Hummingbirds

Her last day on earth
ruby-throated hummingbirds
buzzed the feeder all day long.
We set it up next to the window
where she could see them from her bed.

After her last breath left
and the nice folks from the funeral home
had taken her body away,
those of us still alive noticed
the hummingbirds were gone.

They never came back.
Which reminded me of what the Aztecs said,
that hummingbirds are the spirits
of the dead, come to guide
the wanderer to her home.

She would have been surprised to see them all
in glittering emerald, iridescent ruby
instead of the loose white robes and big white wings
that she expected—her husband Elbert,
saintly mother Loretta, Ruth and Reva
amid a whirring flock of sisters.

But she, who set little store by looks,
would have recognized them anyway.
Even the most unlikely of the lot—
her father Amos Walter, backwoods farmer,
logger, drover, sawmill hand
who ended his rough-hewn days
singing from a shape-note hymn book
I'll Fly Away.

III. Scherzo

My Name is Mud

"Marlboro," a classy English name
graces America's best-selling cigarette.
But a real Anglo-Saxon might, with some regret,

inform you that *marl* means "clay,"
the place where this product
will place you some day.

And *boro* is Olde English, meaning "town."
So Marlboro's really the same name, say,
as Georgia's red-mud, red-neck Clayton.

Mix Saxon marl with snooty French
and now we're in Mudville,
hamlet of the basest ball,

burg bereft of joy or cheer
since Casey at the Bat was smoked
by the least Lucky Strike of all.

And so, beneath our thin veneers,
spattered by sludge
or scrubbed behind the ears,

we're all alike under the skin,
and even the hapless Mudville Nine
are really the Marlboro Men.

Un-Romantic

We might have spoken a language
smooth and sinuous as sheets of satin.
Romantic, like French or Italian
or Spanish—love children of Latin.

However, historical forces
gave us this Germanic gift of gab
which Voltaire, that clever French crab,
compared to the snorting of horses.

Le Tour C'est Fini

On the Tour's final day
we glide down the Champs-Élysée:
Elysian Fields, a picnic in the park
spinning around the Arch of Triumph
under the golden gaze of Joan of Arc.

The last Sunday in July.
Come Monday and August
every Tour-iste knows
all of France will be dark and closed.

If someone you love
is suffering, by chance
withdrawal from the Tour de France,
pining for the snow-capped Alps,
the sunflower fields, the old chateaux,
here is the way to help your beau:

Put on your brightest yellow shirt,
the color of sunshine in Provence
as well as the winner's jersey.
Kiss him or her on both cheeks
(this always works like a cinch)
and whisper endearments in their ear
in any language you like,
as long as it's French.

Now It Can Be Told

While the Germans had their Enigma,
French Underground smugglers in WWII
were given a code by the Brits
to cover the contraband in their boats.

"G" cargo was guns, as one might guess.
Exiles escaped as "E" cargo.
"C" cargo was champagne and cigarettes.
And French snails, of course, were "S" cargo.

Why Do Fashion Models Frown?

You'd think they would smile
like the people who sell us toothpaste,
wrinkle cream, or Cadillacs.
But no, these frowning *fashionistas*
are not *simpático*, not your friends.

Among macaques, gorillas, and baboons
you'll see that identical glare:
"I am the dominant male or female,"
says that relentless glower.
Lesser monkeys must look away,
grin sheepishly and cower.

The model's stare
is printed on the page.
He or she can keep it up for hours.
We the living lack their powers,
must avert our eyes at last.

They do not approve of you.
They belong to a club
you are not a member of,
a clique you can never join.
Unless…

Perhaps if you wore that watch,
those shoes, that skimpy bathing suit—
perhaps you might get more nuts and fruit,
be chased less often, allowed to copulate.

Perhaps you might become one of Them.
Perhaps, at last, they'd smile.

Down on the Sea

Will you stop that incessant pounding?
I've heard your tiresome argument
a thousand times before:

Might makes right!
is all you seem to roar
till you're blue in the face.

You *might* be right,
but you certainly are a bore,
forever foaming at the mouth

with flying spittle. Now please
could we have some quiet,
just a little?

Hearing Aids

After years of increasing quiet
they're back with a vengeance:
the snakelike hiss and slither
of shirtsleeves and sheets of paper
the crinkle of candy wrappers
like icebergs calving
the scritch and scrape
the crunch and crumble
of fallen leaves underfoot.

Drops no longer drip, they trickle.
Even the gently burbling brook
clinks like a jar of pennies
spilling out on a hardwood floor.
The kitchen faucet's crashing roar
like Niagara on the sink'll
make you deaf if you weren't before.
And—dare we say it?—
there's a whole new wrinkle
to that old expression, "Take a tinkle."

Infernal Regions

Reading Dante's *Inferno*
in Fort Worth, Texas,
I looked up and saw a snake
winding its way up the walk
to where I was sitting on the steps.

Then, in the thorn bush beside me,
like little Miss Muffet, I spied
a big hairy spider, sitting
right next to my face.

"Yep," I said to myself.
"This is the place."

The Pluto Society

My ancient home is up there on South Mountain.
—Tao Yuan-ming

Tao, the ancient farmer-poet
always knew where he'd be planted,
his grave among ancestral tombs
the one solid fact in this transitory life.

Uprooted city folks
shorn of all semblance of solidity
instead get letters like this:
The Pluto Society, it seems
wants to cremate me, for free!

But how could they do this for every body,
short of a nuclear conflagration?
Oh, I see. I won't get torched
unless I win a lottery.
Well, that just burns me up.

Still, the thought has some appeal:
a gas grill wafting aloft
my last earthly offering—to what?
No gods (not even Pluto, pissed
at being demoted from a planet)
are waiting to sniff this barbecue.

A toast to the universe, then,
recycling my oxygen and CO_2
for the ecosphere to breathe again
and green leaves sprout anew.

So modern, yet so ancient too—
I could join the countless millions
of Hindus taking their final fling
into the Ganges. Viking kings
setting forth in flaming ships.

When life's little sparrow
has left the building
I could end my days like Beowulf,
smoke from my funeral pyre
rising up into the haze.

Minus his wailing Geats, of course.
Minus the mountainous barrow.
Minus the horsemen galloping around it,
singing songs of praise.

Last Judgment

The moment I've dreaded is here at last,
only it's even worse—
Giving St. Peter a coffee break,
God Himself is flipping through my file!

"A poet?" Storm clouds gather
under those bushy gray brows.
"Lord knows, David
could use some help up here—
I'm getting sick of Psalms."

"Frustrated musician?"
He smiles. "Never could
get the hang of the harp, Myself."

"Aha! An editor!" His eyes light up
with glee. That's something We
can really get Our teeth into!"
He pulls out a pair of golden scales
marked *Joy* and *Pain*, and weighs
the molehill of acceptances I've sent
against the mountain of rejections.

I think of the Book of the Dead
where the Egyptian goddess Maat
weighs the soul, laden with sin,
against a feather.
The light-hearted move on to bliss.
A hippo with a lion's head
is waiting for the heavies.

One pan of the scale sinks down.
God shakes his long white locks
in disbelief. "I guess the joys
were more intense." He shrugs.

"Oh well, let's get on to the good stuff!"
I wince in advance. All those relationships
I slighted for my art! I'm sure they're what
God really cares about. As if to confirm my fears
He gives me a keen and penetrating glance—
"You know, I'm really, *really* into Hearts!"

Not, He's quick to add, the Aztec kind,
still bloody and beating from human sacrifice.
"Yeesh! Gives me the willies!"
Nor yet those sticky-sweet, romantic Valentines.

No—turns out He really, *really* loves
the kind of Hearts you play on a computer!
"*Best thing you ever did,* I told Bill Gates
a few thousand souls ago."
While a line stretching halfway to infinity
shuffles and grumbles and shifts,
He recalls all my wildest, most reckless hands.

"Remember that game against the Red Baron,
the card-counting German guy?
You were online, close to midnight,
both of you north of 90 points, the Korean
and the Spaniard dropped out long ago.
At last you decided to risk everything—
held onto your hearts and the evil Queen,
disguised your intentions to the bitter end—
and then blew him out of the water!"

He chuckles, but then looks askance. "You know,
I could use a guy like you up here. My own Son,
if you can believe it, says that Hearts is sinful—
greedy, scheming, malicious—the very opposite
of everything He stands for. *Christ,
it's just a game!* I tell Him.

"Frankly, I'm worried, Dan, about losing
my edge. All the card-counters, of course,
go straight to the Other Place. Satan stays sharp
by playing your Red Baron every day—
you know the guy had a heart attack
that night you shot the moon.
Been praying for vengeance ever since.

"Come to think of it, well...."
He whistled for St. Pete to watch the gate.
"What say we slip down to Limbo, son,
and take on the team from Hell?"

Redemption

My mom, like many a 50s housewife, collected
S&H Green Stamps at the grocery store,

pasted them into books and turned them in
for toasters, lamps, and other useful stuff.

So, when I thought I'd had about enough,
I went down to the store and said,

"I understand you can redeem
your toils and pains for prizes."

"Yes, it's true," they told me,
handing me a sheaf of empty pages.

"All you have to do
is fill this book."

IV. A Date with Clio

Muse of History

Tough as Nails

One thing for sure about cave men
(and no doubt about cave females)
that everyone has somehow overlooked—
they *hated* their fingernails.

No nail clippers way back then.
What did they do? Wear them down,
like rodents' teeth, by digging roots?
Or, despite the dirt and filth,
just chew and chew and chew?

Forget about Cave Bears and Dire Wolves
and other horrific tales—
the biggest source of Stone Age stress
was *fingernails*.

No one can bear to live with a ragged

                              nail—

think about having all ten
as jagged as the HiMAlAyAs.
It's even annoying typographically.
Nails scraping across the chalkboard of history
don't even begin to describe it.

Nature, red in tooth, was at her worst
when it came to the human claw.
Less of a talon than a flake, too flimsy
to oppose a Sabertooth, all you could do
was wait for it to break.

Surely those designers of fur *couture*,
those tamers of raging fire,

did *something* to alleviate their ire
about our all-too-human flaw.
At the risk of speaking out of school,
I'd say that axes, knives, and arrowheads
were not our first and most important tool.

Despite his reputation as a boor
a real cave man, I think we can be sure
was prone to spend his nights around the fire
cracking jokes and marrow bones,
swapping tales of shaggy mastodons
while, with a slender file of finest stone
carefully buffing his manly manicure.

1200 BC

The Hittites

The Hittites took an innocent delight
in hitting people.
They wondered why their neighbors
looked so glum.
What could be more fitting, or more fun
than being hit by Hittites?

They loved to bash the Babylonians
and cane the Canaanites.
Their charitable activities
included ramming Rameses.

Alas, their cracks went over like a ton
of sun-baked bricks. From Troy to Sumer
no one in the ancient Middle East
shared their sense of humor in the least.

It puzzled them, this lack of fans
among Phoenicians and Assyrians.
Why, pray, did those Bronze Age louts
all pray to Baal to bail them out?

Why, when they came out to play
did everybody turn around and run?
You'd almost think that folks could hardly wait
for the Empire of the Hittites to be done.

340 BC

His story

Before Alexander was Great, he did excel
at playing the flute. Philip of Macedon,
that brute, would scold at his son:
"Music is a woman's work!
Are you not ashamed to play so well?"

So Alex went into a line of work
on which history loves to dwell:
slaughtering armies, conquering kings,
trading his flute for the war horn
with it brassy bray and swell.

The moon on a cliff above the Aegean Sea.
Healing and nurturing, giving birth.
Feeding and clothing humanity.
The pure silver stream of a single flute—
of these, history does not tell.

793 AD

Lindisfarne

*Anno dccxciii: Dire portents were seen over the Northumbrian land...
huge flashes of light, and flaming dragons flying through the sky... that
same year, on the sixth of the Ides of June, a raid by heathen men destroyed,
with looting and manslaughter, God's church upon the isle of Lindisfarne.*
—*Anglo-Saxon Chronicle*

Thank the Lord you've found this letter
here where I've hidden it under the altar stones
just moments before they come.

Thor's hammer
will soon be knocking at Christ's door.
The greatest pleasure
of these sons of Cain, I hear
is bashing out human brains.

I know my brothers
will die like loyal servants of our Lord,
defending with bare hands and heads
our relics and manuscripts.
God help me, but I
have a sturdy iron crucifix
and I intend to use it.

Beneath this letter, in a wooden box
you'll find a manuscript.
A foolish, idle work of mine
called *Beowulf.* About a time
when even pagan kings knew honor
and the strongest man on this middle earth
was also the kindest and most generous.

Those days are gone.
Perhaps they never were.
The brothers are huddled here in prayer.
We hear a distant shouting on the shore.

Be well, my friend.
May you live in better times than these.
Ave atque vale.

8OO AD

Suspense

The Anglo-Saxons, like children
unused to the tense demands
of literary art, the wily craft
of word-weaving artisans,
needed the poet to hold their hands.

Fear not, sang the Saxon *scop*
as Grendel crept into the hall
and devoured a sleeping Geat
tendons and bones and all
right down to his hands and feet.

"Fear not the deafening din
of mead benches slamming the wall,
the soul-chilling screams of agony—
mankind's great hero, Beowulf
is doomed to win."

We now consider it a lack of art
to give away the end before the start.
Having drunk the nectar of the Muse
so long and deep, we need
stronger stuff than Saxon honey mead.

Back then, in the childhood of our kind
monsters lurked in every swamp and fen.
Life was brutal, terror stark.
In our brightly lit world we forget
how afraid we once were of the dark.

No wonder, as Professor Alfred said,
the Saxons saw something lurking
behind every bush and under every bed.
Their word for Fate was *Weird*
and doom hung by a thread.

Their world was wild and muddy,
not paved and fenced and neat.
Wiser, perhaps, than we are,
they knew that our long, dark struggle
might still end in defeat.

1660 AD

Enlightenment Man

The Royal Society
thought they were smart
for getting together
to take him apart.

Will all the King's horses
and all the King's men
ever put Humpty
together again?

1819 AD

Vale of Soles

The path along Peachtree Creek is soft
and sandy in the springtime. Filtered sun
brings out the blonde color, and the tracks
of shoe sole hieroglyphics written there—
myriad patterns, as different as fingerprints
diffract the light. I add mine to the mix, a palimpsest
that rubber soles rub out and write anew.

Some are cheap old sneakers,
some sleek running shoes. They're all
about the same at what they do—
give us some traction in the sand,
help us to hold our ground.

Keats could have used
a pair of these, to write his name
if not on water, then at least
upon these not so lone and level sands.
Pious folks ask, What would Jesus do?
I'd rather ponder, What would Keats
have worn? I'll bet,

the cheapest, plainest sneaker he could get—
black canvas with white rubber soles.
The name would appeal to him: *Converse,*
for *conversation,* for doing the exact *reverse*
of what most people do.

For chasing nightingales, they'd work as well
as some designer shoe, expensive, hip.
Money won't buy you a perfect purchase here,
as poets have always said, for what it's worth.

Sooner or later, our soles always lose their grip.
Sooner or later, we all slip and fall off the earth.

2018 AD

Surprised

Just got the news today—
Surprised by Joy is now defunct.
Surveying the current scene
one can't be too surprised at this—
little poetry magazines
are daily being born and dying.
But was this a natural death?

Two possibilities come to mind:
Is Joy so universal now
no one is surprised to see her?
Seems improbable, somehow.
More likely, our current Triumvirate—
Donald, Ryan, Mitch McConnell—
has outlawed her altogether.

Poor Joy—I knew her
in my youth, back in the 60s.
She liked to hang out with Peace and Love.
A faerie, floating thing,
she seemed to have no needs
beyond a bunch of flowers
and perhaps a string of beads.

Like many another refugee,
like polar bears and coral reefs,
she suffered when the climate changed,
the flower children overthrown
by Big Oil and Money Men,
by former Christians making friends
with Hatred, War, and Greed.

Poor Joy. I've been surprised
how much I miss her quiet voice,
her gentle grace. Now anger
begets anger, hatred hate,
and the lambs of God are being led
unto the slaughter. Will we ever
see her lovely face again?

Now

Be Here Then

Nobody knows the Now.
Just as the light from some exploding star
dawns upon our eyes a billion years
after the actual event,
so light from the nearest leaf
also takes its own sweet time
to reach us. Slower still,
bankers in the back room of our eyes
exchange those photons
for electric current, golden coin
of the realm we call the brain.

Besieged by a billion bits of news,
cutting and pasting at lightning speed,
the mind now edits and directs
that moving and compelling picture show
we call "reality." The world we see,
though not what it appears to be,
is even more of a miracle than we think.

True, the Now is where we live
and breathe, and have our being.
But no matter how fast we run
it always eludes our grasp.
All of our knowing and seeing
remains but a shadow of Plato's fire,
forever rooted in the past.

V. A Sprinkling of *Elephant Water*

Elephant Water

I've never seen an elephant so old.
Her face is freckled with age marks, pink and brown.
But there's more to her than her wrinkled dignity:
When the little one carefully put his front knees
In the water, she ran up and butted him in.

Now, when she lifts her trunk from the pond
The little kids jump back and scream,
Thinking
She may have something more in mind
Than drinking.

As for me, a Southern Baptist bred
I too was always taught to avoid a sprinkling.
"Full immersion or nothing!" they always said.

But the old beguiler gets around my doubts—
If only she would spout
That blessing that the children hope and fear
I'd throw myself into that shower.

Cool and alive from the elephant's trunk,
I think of a drop of it sitting on my palm.
We wait for that animal water, long and long....

Her trunk swings down.
She fooled us all.
It was nothing… then,
Too late, I see that a trick
Has taken me in.

Long after the children leave
I'm still standing there
Immersed in the ponderous, graceful air
And a drop of elephant water.

In Honor of Roaches

Man is no doubt a higher being
But I'm one who can't get used to seeing
The results of my bug-spray genocide.

Their limbs so decently tucked in,
No malice in their form or face:
It eases my conscience that one decides
On a dish for his final resting place.

Clean china, white: in no way narrow
The spirit of this little hero
Who chose the funeral of a Pharaoh.

"Small Beowulf," the dragon sighed,
"The honor is all with those who died."
And though I'll have to wash the plate
I don't regret that you lie in state.

Egret

A slip of a thing
as slender as thought
an almost remembered word
a dream that the morning forgot.
Edgewise in the thin, sunny air
it shimmers and disappears
long legs, long neck
long beak.

Stretched between heaven and earth
like an angel in penance
it ekes
out a living
stalking about in the mud.

Craning its neck
it listens
for the call,
the summons back,
the tiny suitcase
of its body
always packed
with a pair
of enormous white wings.

Wear and Tear

the poet to his underwear

What is this, underwear?
This sudden fragile, antique, ghostly air
Fade far away, dissolve, and quite forget....
Is this what you've gotten from hanging around with poets?

I know,
It's no fun being sat on.
But listen,
You're not that much holier than me
And here I am after all these years
Still clinging to the bottom of society.
If I can do it, so can you—
Hang in there!

Please, underwear
Don't give up on this veil of tears
And leave me behind all cold and bare!
Don't listen to those nightingales—
I need you!

The Middle of the Day

The morning of life is gone.
Its level light
Has lifted, and the sun
Now beats upon our backs.
The owl, too wise
To venture out into the heat
Awaits the dusk
For its soft flight.
Children and animals sleep,
Leaving the field, all dry and bare
To us.
This is our time.
O Lord, I pray
Be with us all who labor
In the middle of the day.

Alligator Pond

St. Petersburg, Florida

Bubbles…
The breath of a fish?
Or marsh gas,
Something rotting in the muck beneath.
Bubbles…
The only sign of life in this grey-green swamp
Here on this heavy, humid afternoon
Where the hand of time has stopped at three o'clock
Where the blood, too tired to move
Drains to the feet
And Death, that low-pressure salesman
Sets up shop.

The surface is unruffled, calm and still
As the tar pits at La Brea,
That ancient Mesozoic tourist trap
Whose sticky, oleaginous black underneath
Was hidden by a slick of drinking water
Concealing from unwary mastodons
Or sabertooths, or such newfangled beasts
The dinosaur's revenge.

The old order is alive and well. It waits
In these out-of-the-way cafés
Where the service is heavy and slow
The way they used to do business
Back in the dinosaur days.

The alligator, analog
Of Death, waits sleepily
The shutters of his eyes
Half open. Cradled

In the ancient grisly soup
His rock
Is one of ages. Eons roll
In the quiet blinking of an eye.
Heavy and slow, the undertaker
And the undertow, he waits.

The café is quiet for the afternoon.
There will be customers,
Never fear. Not, perhaps
Today, this week. But
Soon enough. He grins
An archaic grin.

His brother down below,
The snapping turtle, also waits.
Planted in ooze, he sits
Silt-covered, jagged as a rock.
Jaws open, with a look of gruesome bliss
He wiggles
His little pink lure,
Angling for ducklings,
Curious, silver fish—
Anything more anxious, more impatient,
More alive. All things come
To him who waits, and waits....

Bubbles appear
In the heavy afternoon....
The only sign of life in this grey-green swamp
Where the hand of time has stopped at three o'clock
Where the blood, too tired to move
Drains to the feet
And Death, that low-pressure salesman
Sets up shop.

Elegy for the Age of Oil

Junkyard, Soddy Daisy, Tennessee

You old jalopies,
Hot rods, pickup trucks—
No more
Dinosaur juice for you.
No more that rich, intoxicating brew
Of club moss, ferns, huge joints
Of brontosaurus meat
With pterodactyl bones
Thrown in for flavor.
No more firewater.
Some of you
Were kindly drunks, no doubt,
Purring like kittens.
Some, when tanked up, roared
Like your ancestral dragons, fumed,
Bellowed black smoke, and belched
Pipeloads of half-digested gas.
Alas, no more.
No more
Tyrannosaurus.
Only
Wrecks.

Age of Information

We dream of a paperless society,
of information pristine, clean
as snow-melt on the mountains.
Only the pure can hope to pass
through the needle's eye
of a fiber optic cable—only signal,
not one single bit or byte of noise.

The Age of Paper was filthy
rich with dirty information.
Handwriting would always betray
your character and state of mind:
John Hancock's signature told King George
that he faced a determined man.
From awkward youth to palsied age,
the body was always gossiping behind your hand,
saying more than you wanted to say.

Eager to learn our secrets,
paper soaked up everything
that came its way.
Oil of your skin
left fingerprints
more truly yours
than any signature.
Coffee stains bespoke
a sleepy editor,
lipstick a lover.

No impression
was too faint to save.
A delicate perfume
would sometimes drift up from the envelope,
a séance with a medium

that spoke to us
beyond the grave.

Something only you could give
went into everything you wrote—
long, dark, lustrous strands of you
would lie concealed
within the locket of a letter,
microscopic flakes of skin,
stray eyelash, private pubic curl,
perhaps a drop of sweat, a tear—
all carefully sealed up
(appalling as this may appear)
with your saliva.

This is my body,
written for you—
break open,
read.

Sometimes noise
can be a signal of its own—
the "snow" on TV sets turned out
to be the Big Bang's lingering radiance,
a broadcast of the birthday of the universe.

Just so, all those useless bits,
those flakes of us that fell
on the Age of Paper like an endless snow
concealed in code
the deepest secret that we have to tell—
a store of information so complete
that future scholars, archeologists,
can reconstruct the sender
cell by cell.

The Seal

You body forth the shape of things unseen
Working in flesh
A line of forebears labored
To express the heart's desire
They could not speak,
Apprenticed to the slow and patient task
Of bending bone

The master artist and the masterpiece
In you their embodied longing can be seen
Gliding at ease in your well-loved element
At home, at last
In the dark shape of your dream

My Long Thigh Bone

I'm dancing to the Supremes while making dinner
When I happen to look at my dolphin bone—
I found it down on the beach's rocks
A long curved bone
It reminds me of the long curved backs of dolphins
As they roll up out of the sea.
I look down at my long thigh bone
And wonder if anyone will think of me
When I dance my way into archaeology
And all the music left is in my bones—
I wonder, will anyone see this bone and dream
Of the way I used to dance to the Supremes?

Dan Veach is the founder and for two decades the editor of *Atlanta Review*. His collection of poems and Chinese ink paintings, *Elephant Water*, won the Georgia Author of the Year Award. Dan's translations from Chinese, Arabic, Spanish, and Anglo-Saxon have won the Willis Barnstone Translation Prize and the Independent Publisher Book Award. He is the editor and co-translator of *Flowers of Flame: Unheard Voices of Iraq* (Michigan State University Press, 2008). A recipient of the Georgia Writers Lifetime Achievement Award, Dan has performed his poetry worldwide, including Oxford University, People's University in Beijing, the American University in Cairo, the Atheneum in Madrid, and the Adelaide Festival in Australia. He also plays bass clarinet and composes for concert band and orchestra.

www.ingramcontent.com/pod-product-compliance
Lightning Source LLC
Chambersburg PA
CBHW031358060726
47590CB00007B/2838